ETTEILLA

OR

THE ONLY TRUE WAY

TO DRAW

THE CARDS

An English translation of the original book in French

Translation by
Marius Høgnesen

ORIGINAL TITLE IN FRENCH:

ETTEILLA,

OU LA SEULE MANIERE DE TIRER LES CARTES,

REVUE, CORRIGEE ET AUGMENTEE

PAR L'AUTEUR;

SUR SON PREMIER MANUSCRIT.

PUBLISHED IN 1773

THIS BOOK WAS A REISSUE, AN EXPANDED EDITION OF JEAN-BAPTISTE ALLIETTE'S OR ETTEILLA'S FIRST BOOK FROM 1770; *ETTEILLA, OU MANIERE DE SE RECREER AVEC UN JEU DE CARTES PAR M.* * * * (ETTEILLA, OR A WAY TO ENTERTAIN YOURSELF WITH A PACK OF CARDS FOR M. * * *)

Playing card Images: Copyright © JC. Flornoy Estate. www.tarot-history.com

Book published by:
https://www.circleandtriangle.com

ISBN: 978-82-692706-2-4 PAPERBACK
ISBN: 978-82-692706-3-1 EBOOK

TRANSLATOR'S NOTE

Jean-Baptiste Alliette was born in Paris in 1738 and died during the onset of the French Revolution in 1791. He was the first author to publish works on card divination and was in his time considered quite the occultist. His pseudonym Etteilla was simply his surname reversed. His books on the Tarot, and in particular his own Tarot deck; the Grand Etteilla, is read and used still to this day. His books, this being his first, also influenced many later occultists, such as Papus and Arthur Edward Waite.

Whatever one may think of Etteilla, whether a street hustler or a genuine occult seeker, his ideas have influenced the way we read the cards today. In order to make Etteilla more accessible to more people, I have felt it important to translate this book from French to English. I have illustrated this book with all the original card spreads. The card images are the Provot from the 1790s and have been provided by Flornoy. Moreover, to help the reader, navigate the text, I have also provided several explanatory foot notes for easy reference. Enjoy the read!

MARIUS HØGNESEN

TO MADAME,

THE DUCHESS OF * * *.

MADAME,

You will be, I believe, rather surprised by the request that I make to you today. I ask you to accept the dedication of this small first print edition. I should be the last person articulating the letters, the initials of your last name and title, but by the same token you were the person inquiring into my Oracle combinations, which are based on the sublime science of numbers. With your permission, Madame, please accept my homage. In gratitude. I will not even try to praise your illustrious and respectable genealogy, nor your personal merits. I do not dare to undertake it. Many are the famous writers who have more worthily consecrated these to the temple of memory. I will but limit myself to admire in silence how far the goodness of the people of your rank go, and acknowledge a descendant of one of the greatest men of the last century. I have the honor to remain in deep respect,

MADAME,

Your very humble and obedient servant,
ETTEILLA.

FIRSTLY
IN GENERAL
Pertaining to the Art of Divination[1].

We have always contemplated facts, but the reference back to the divinatory science that found them has often been overlooked. I can talk on this at length, because I have applied myself to follow with a critical mind the writings of all the ancient and modern authors, who have spoken for or against it.

The issue is, whether there are or have been diviners, and if it is permitted and indeed possible to predict future events. I have found, that the most knowledgeable and the most philosophical ones, each have a feeling of being in the right, but after having supported a certain point of view,

---

[1] Translator: Please note, the 1770 book edition is identical to the 1773 edition except for this section covering the art of divination.

often end up adopting another. What I have noticed with many of these authors, is the perpetuation or exaggeration of the misconceptions, indeed contradictions in the very same book. This I find absolutely appalling, to condemn with fire what they confess to want to permit, if only we could take a more subtle approach. From the point of view of a Practitioner, let us please discuss the substance of the issue.

Is there any real harm in being a cartomancer?[2] Yes, if the Horoscope-Maker is a treacherous, lurking impostor, a sordid soul, a bad citizen, surely too, the cartomancer is a man to be banished from society, and even to be punished as soon as we have proof, not of what he has predicted through cartomancy; but with the view, he has abused the trust of his clients. And we must also contemplate whether this cartomancer, who appears to be guilty, is indeed so; because as a reflective man, I say in general, that when a prejudice is laid against someone, false

---

[2] Translator; the word used for cartomancer in the original text in French is *Geneliate*.

allegations often emerge to put him on trial[3]; but if this cartomancer is recognized as an upright gentleman, a proud and virtuous politician, not looking so much for a prognostication, but by the good understanding of his fellows, Oh! Then, we find our rebuttals, obliged to lower their arms. But then, they say, the cartomancer has now ceased to be one. In my case, I certify, on the contrary, that he is more than ever a cartomancer, worthy of men, and of his name. If he is honest, the prognostication will be clear of iniquity: if he is wise, his Oracles will all hold weight, be measured and have sound reflections. If he is a virtuous politician, he does not, will not condemn, with a raised eyebrow the flaws of men; but will wish to see a change in the dreadful behavior they have, he will gradually bring them back to good, with his wise and skillful foresight. In short, he loves the virtuous, helps society, and will cement in silence this or that, what ten established families could not do with great effort.

---

[3] We have killed more than one, who, far from being a Sorcerer, better described as a detective, as witnessed by Joan of Arc, with two or three hundred others.

Example. The wise and learned cartomancer says: I respect your free will, Heaven protects you; however, with Mercury dominant in the sign of Aquarius etc., at the moment of your birth, this assures me that you will receive such and such news, and it just happens, that this time is tomorrow.

The announcement is effective, for whatever reason the sage or the critic wishes to admit. In the end, a certain confidence of hope is established in the consultant, and the cartomancer, a truly honest-man, takes advantage of this disposition and the circumstances to cement peace and good resolutions.

But since I know better than our theorists, the strength and weaknesses of divination, and what this science contains of just and unjust, I do encourage absolutely a thorough testing out of the cartomancer. It can only do a good for society that one can assess, whether a cartomancer is this by name only, and thus a bad citizen and would cause all sorts of ailments.

I will not bring forth any examples of those I have known and seen, I even in protest must keep silent about, the track record of these numerous predictions, where evil diviners, by their poisonous tongues, have caused irreparable damage. But as, according to two authors, the Savant la Mothe Le Vayer assures us, that God does allow there to be diviners. It is however to be desired that these cartomancers apply it with conscience, in a tender and noble way, without which, instead of doing good, they would only ready tyrants to devour each other. But, says a fair man: We should generally expel all those who get involved in prognostication, as we have done in the past, on pain of death or banishment. I answer, that the laws are explicit in this regard; but when it does happen, did you not feel that a higher power had some root in it? And have we not also seen the wise be sacrificed instead of the guilty? It is but important to recognize and not to mistake the science of cartomancy from the ignorant cartomancer; the latter has a sordid and wicked soul; he follows the inclinations of his consultant in order to be better paid. But the real cartomancer is very different; he accepts, that which must be.

II

Let us return to this serious defense which, without destroying the entire category of such men, would force the wise cartomancer, subjected to the laws of his existing Prince, to reserve in his bosom a science, which he would not be able to use, to use only for the sole purpose of pleasing; however, if carried out would expel the real cartomancer; he would revive a crowd of greedy souls, whom light punishment, proportionate to the fault of the offence, would never be granted.

Let us leave the good and the evil as is, supporters leave the above point of view, and advise the seeker to think twice before questioning a genius, who may be a scientist or an ignoramus; but if curiosity guides man, may he be careful not to give to the weak creature, what is absolutely reserved for the Divine Creator, and with this fundamental point in mind, let him think like me on this subject, when speaking to a cartomancer. You have a certain talent an 'Art of prognostication', this you should commit to; work on the past and the present, and we will judge your science of the future.

This foreword leads me to report this incident:

» Tyrtamus, a Doctor cartomancer having come » from Africa to Athens, with all the reputation of » a great man of palmistry of sorts, Socrates to » trap him, had made a precise print of one of his » hands, all the features and lines, and sent » this with one of his disciples, with instructions » to say, that the figure or print was from the » hand of a woman. The savant Tyrtamus knew it » was of a man, and moreover one prone to theft; » which was heard and met with disdain reactions » towards the Doctor cartomancer; however the » wise Socrates confessed, that he indeed was » inclined to such a vice, and that reason alone » had prevented it. » O free will! You see, the correct prognostication rendered with all the forces of divination, your higher power as determined by the arrangement of the stars at the time of your birth.

Si quis majus quam sapientia humana velit consequi, divinationi det operam, necesse est.

If someone wants more than human wisdom and experience, give necessary attention to divination.

This Sentence from the same Socrates has struck me ever since my youth. I have looked for all the opportunities to see and to know the men who possessed this sublime divinatory science, in order to become a diviner myself. But having found in my country only madmen or ignorant people, I undertook to go and look for these doctors in distant lands, only to encounter in vast quantities the so-called Soothsayers, Wizards, Enchanters and Magicians, mere blind men, equally credulous types, the Inept, the Enthusiasts, the Lazy, the Bums, Cunning folk, the wicked, rascals and the likes. So in this way I distinguished only two classes of men. The first holding a rank in society, and the last being what is called the dregs of the people, people without fortune, without education, without morals. What contrast!

Introduced into the midst of these, I embarrassed myself in the traps they normally lay out for anyone, who presents themselves to them; but discovering their fraud, I proved to them that simple Magic, natural or artificial, had produced everything. It is presumed that in researching this celestial science, I encountered more dangers than insights; however I feared the former less than I valued the latter. In a sentence, I sought and I wanted to find. Denmark, Russia, Turkey, Poland, Prussia, Germany, Hungary, Spain, Italy, Sardinia, Piedmont and France itself, were more then, than today filled with such people. Caves and dungeons were not exempt either. Some were for the fortunes; others for the fame; some for the leisure; others for the connections. What madness! Etteilla saw all these men, he followed them, stayed with them; but none seem to him to possess this great divinatory knowledge; he despite of this did not doubt that it existed; Socrates, the old wise man, attests to this reality; he also reflected on the clear prognostications of Anaximander, Spirink, Asclerarion, Adrien du Dicius, la Case, Plotinus, Gauric, Richard Gervin, Louis de Farnese, Lucius Bellancius, and whatever may or can be said of the critics, they do still reflect on the learned, with many centuries of Mr. Nostradamus. It goes far beyond still; he sees that there have indeed been diviners. What perplexity! Where to find them if they still exist? After all, did the sages take care in imposing this knowledge on posterity? Pythagoras, Aristotle, Tacitus and many others, did they all want to be imposters, or were perhaps men with ailments. A few authors see the point in maintaining that there can be no such diviners, however do we need to believe them?

Regardless, Etteilla, regretful to have reached the age of twenty-one, without having made other discoveries, than that of a thousand people as useless as they are unworthy of the words of the sage, indulged himself yet again, reading a number of authors, who were not in agreement with the ancient Philosophers, in whether this was an acquired knowledge, or an infused gift of guessing, therefore drowned this divine knowledge in a jumble of absurdities. Such are the works by Parascelle, Prellus, Porphirius, Jamblichus, Proclus, Cornellius, Agrippa, Wierianno and others who don't offer credulous work, just the appearances of truth, and never the same truth. He also read the books, that were said to be by Honorius .... of Leon .... the foolishness of the Author Anonymous, of little Albert, as well as the so-called books of Salomon, every day new nonsense was added. However, as Etteilla believed to be able to find in this maze of impertinences, at least one path which could lead to the Temple of Truth, the only goal of his research, he operated thus all the more justly, because he knew better how to interpret the meanings of the scriptures, than many of these men of all types and ages, most of whom, were unaware of the science of scrutinizing to the letter, what he had seen a hundred times at work.

Furious at having, like most of them, wasted the remainder of his heritage, without having discovered anything, he resumed traveling the countryside with the intention of finding these so-called Soothsayers, or at least to find some real ones, if there were any. The human weakness! This journey as fruitless as the first, and which led him only to be convinced of the deceit of some, and the stupidity of others.

At the age of twenty-nine, finally back in his native home, he read through and re-compiled an innumerable collection of secrets, recipes and thoughts, that he had carefully assembled; but he did not find anything, but a confused mass of repetitions, of nonsense, some false, and other useless.

A middle-aged man advised him to read the rebuttals of the Protestant Bekker, which appeared to be based on very vain principles; for after all, it may be something, but this author maintains that it is nothing, and in this he disagrees with L. Lavatere, also a protestant minister in Zurich, and who lived a hundred and twenty years before his successor. He read Jean Bodin, he judged him more bigoted than Jurisconsulte[4]; he went through the works of Delancre; he considered it more suited to be buried in solitude, than to have been dedicated to one of our Kings: through Martin Delrios, he found these magical controversies[5] well worthy to be put on the fire, and the author of Extravagances (by M. Ouf, who makes us read a lot of good and bad) who would have had, in Etteilla's opinion, much better results, if he had

---

[4] *Majori electa studio quam scripta judicio.* (Mayor chosen for a study, which had a written judgment)
[5] Too bright.

discussed the causes, instead of worrying about the effects; he would not have missed the mark as he did; for although Etteilla tries to make a fool of his Mr. Ouf, he waxes the authorities that the initiates respect. And I cannot overlook a very gloomy compilation made by de Lisle in 1634, on Talismanic Science, of which the original Author with more absurdity, claims that spaces were seen in fluids.

As a result of all these observations and many others, I was indignant at these writers, so-called Magicians, and I despised all of their stupid or malignant rebuttals.

If I only would stop looking for what the hidden nature of the sage was. In finishing my painful work, I had only halted the storm, which had been gathering above me; but Socrates did not leave my thoughts. I was all in. This embarrassing situation, but again, I was advised to look into sources purer (than I am permitted to say.) Who would have believed it, he who knew me as a fool, a first-rate Enthusiast. You are learned, he said to me, seek the key, you will find what you seek, and you will also find the universal medicine there. I did find it, but not from the arena of these persistent impostors. I repeat, I searched, and I found. The dens, the black forests of all the satanic people, had not slowed down my desire. It wasn't that I was more reckless than the next; but it is, like I said before, because I was mad enough to seek at the risk of my life, the delights of being educated. I did not live, and my life was spared. Yes, of course, I can affirm that there was never a man who pushed further than me. The frantic desire to find what we call Magic Art; four or five hundred leagues at distance, in order to see a so-called Soothsayer or Sorcerer, did not stop me. To achieve this, I repeatedly experienced all the fatigue, humiliation and human misfortunes; a traveler without fortune has. I walked during the day, at the mercy of the inclement of the seasons, and I stopped at night without wanting to wait, to shelter, to rest. By doing so, I had lost everything and found nothing, almost like the pilot-less ship, which is at the mercy of the winds and the waves, which toss it, break it and swallow it up. I had been taken over.

If you are not convinced, some of these men claim maliciously, that they have this so-called science pinned down, or rather only need one piece to achieve it. Go to Etteilla, those who know me will tell them; you will see in him, not a Theoretician, but a Practitioner, a man who, while operating, does not allow himself to be surprised by natural effects, and who does not with the light of a weak lamp acknowledge the mechanical springs of his person, nor controls the operations of his understanding.

All the dark circles invented with the greatest deception, the result of greed by some and the ignorance of others, dazzle me like it must you. I thought I saw, I thought I heard; I, like the madmen of this species, certify that I have seen, in ripe, I have reflected on my fictions, the phantoms given birth by my imagination and have ended up seeing them vanish with the torch light of Wisdom. But if I attack Magic so boldly, it's not that I believe that there is absolutely nothing: there is undoubtedly something, that is all I can say here; and this something is as difficult to discover, as would be, to find a needle in a heap of hay.

So, let's see if such a great seeker[6] of the Magic Arts, who has sought so much and traveled in order to find, to encounter: Indeed, I saw and learned, not of Black Magic, but of simple, natural and artificial Magic. This is the real way to discover in the bowels of Earth, waters and metals, with a wand from the Elbow tree, plucked on the twelfth degree of the September Moon, Natural.

The molten lead thrown in water, the white wax thrown on a black background, the coffee grounds tossed between the cup and the saucer, the egg white, languished with some salt. Artificial.

The ring suspended by a hair in a glass of water; Abstraction. The lock of hair or sieve, or, if you like, the sieve suspended by scissors; Trickery. The key in a Book; if there is no vice, subterfuge. The thirty-three sticks placed in a circle about the height of the chest; Illusions of the ancient Gauls. I say illusions, in that they

---

[6] Translator: The word in the text in French is *Curieux*.

imagined that they actually saw the Soldiers or Generals flee, who they had designated by their sticks, when said sticks left the circle; or if they noticed their stick generals, inferior, they gave victory to the stronger enemy general, whatever was most in fashion. Surely the most useful, (not for the Art of guessing the future, itself contingent) is to seek out what is of the occult and what has some relation to physics.

Let's move on to more interesting ones. First appears before our eyes the very large catalog in the form of the rebuttals of which I have spoken, and which are futile to repeat. Next dominates the famous Electra of steel, having an infinity of angles, which has been the subject to much scrutiny..... This Electra represents the will, the deceased or absent man and so on. The Magic mirror, representing still the thief stealing effects; the rose springing to life from soil in a clear vase, placed on an artificially heated table; the magic tree of real wood, whose vegetation is made visibly by the contrast of hot and cold; the amazing light; the man in trance; the ideal meal; the sheep herded and tranquilized by only one knocking of the crook, the post suddenly stopping, the means of remedying it; the tree that gives wine; bonfire made in a barn full of straw without the danger of fire, and many others, of which I will speak to, or I will demonstrate for free in a few years, if permission is me granted.

So far these secrets have been attributed to the Magic Arts, but are nothing more, as I said, and it bears repeating, they are of very simple nature, natural or artificial, (of such that a Gibeciere-performer would derive great advantage) just witness the skin of a small horse that we refer to as Turkish[7], and an infinity of others, that I will not disclose, in order to give the seeker a more pleasant surprise, who may revere this little course in ideal Magic. But as this surprise will be more pleasant to me than to them, I must say in advance, that I will only perform in public, all that I announce, and I will gain all the more from it,

---

[7] This so-called horse, which appeared in Fairs and on the Boulevards, was nothing more than an imitation of a horse artistically made of cardboard and wood, covered with the skin of such an animal, on which a woman would mount, and which did whatever she made it do, while taking care not to make people discover the trickery. The praise that was given, was not to the talent of the artist, who made it.

since the facts cited are never more impactful, as when they are shown to our very eyes.

It is not with the purpose to cover myself with a mask of deceit, that I single him out; as I have often said in my first edition, and as I will repeat in this one; I am not a Magician; this is a truth that I still attest to in my Mysterious Zodiac, and which was confirmed by the author of the bulletin with the Oracle of that day. Yes, of course, I would be very upset, to even have such a reputation; but I nevertheless dare to say, that I am unique in the accuracy of my predictions: I bet fifty Louis that Madame la Duchesse de *** would give birth to a Prince; the event justified my gamble, as many people can testify to, so money was lavished on me with more joy, than what I could accept. But, seeker hear me, today I predict that a greater Lady, I would say a Princess of my country, will give birth, close to the passing of this year, to a greater Prince; and certainly this prognostication everyone can promote[8]. Do not

---

[8] Translator: If Etteilla was thinking, that Marie Antoinette´s marriage to Louis XVI in 1770 (king 1774-1792) would produce a prince in 1773, he would have been wrong, the couple only produced a princess in 1778 with the birth of Marie-Therese Charlotte.

cry out to Magic! Listen to the lyrics that follow instead. Study nature, says the sage, and you will rise above yourself. Study the little world, since you have not allowed yourself to enter into the realm of the great; weigh, measure, count age, life and related events; laws, carefully, wisely, meditate in secret on what you have to say in public, so when you open your mouth, you will pronounce only Oracles.

It is by following such maxims, in accordance with the experience and the studies that I have explained, that I believe to have brought the Art of Prognostication to its final stage. There is not a general prophecy in Europe, not saying we will see *great turmoil*. It's to one individual to whom I say: *Beware of the number fourteen, ten thousand eyes will be gazing at you.*

And how do I say these things? Not in the manner as those vile men and women, so-called Wizards or Witches, Soothsayers, Magicians, card throwers say: According to one; I don't know who is in our minds... what escapes our mouths. What absurdity! What frivolous answer! Like me, would they not rather say, I say this for the fun of it, as you question me on you; and if you like, we are crazy both; but our follies do not harm anyone: you are a seeker, I call myself a scholar; we deal with each other, and we're happy, although many people may disagree.

But, my friend Etteilla, who picks up a persisting follower; you are going through the countryside, all the while, we have learned that you are saying some amazing things. I see, I reply, what amazes me is you; on what will not happen, please forget it; and on what will happen make stress of it. Spread the rumors of my correct prognostication, and I challenge posterity to either make me into one of the greatest diviners or not; some may even give me a more serious qualification. But I wash my hands of it, and although I am a reflective being and a profound calculator, I do not give my solid combinations only for pleasant pastimes and frivolous amusements.

Now let's challenge those who take me for a motley original, a species of scarecrow; because many people, speaking of Etteilla, make of him, before seeing him, into a frightful phantom, who at least must live with Gnomes. Don't pay any attention to it; I have the same features and the same habitation as the common man; but I only share the art, or rather the gift of deep thinking with a very few. I am certainly not cynical like Diogenes; but I am perhaps thoughtful like the Author of the English Spectator: and if in one word, you will agree, seeing me, I dare not give myself the quality of a diviner, at least I can apply that of a wise man, and the Soothsayer is no more than a sage[9]. I have before said that the price of my consultations is 24 livre, and that of my Horoscopes 50 livre. If this price seems expensive to the public, in general, it cannot be it, take into account in particular the fortunes of my clients, eager to satisfy themselves pleasantly.

Although the man who has the most concerns with consulting the future, he is nevertheless the one who most desires it; this is why he must prefer to have recourse with someone who speaks with an open heart, without charlatanism and without enthusiasm. He will come to see in some of his Oracles, the deep knowledge that Etteilla has of

---

[9] This was an idea conceived by the ancients.

periodic returns, of the perpetual rotations and of the fortuitous sequences of events in human life. But here is the surprise.

Etteilla does not need to see his clients; he wishes neither to speak with them, nor to know them, in order to give them an amusing Horoscope, and sometimes if useful he will also speak of the past, the present and the future, with a precision that may pleasantly surprise them. It suffices for him, as he has already informed the public, to receive on a piece of paper the initial letters of the clients name (without the need for any information of title or family), the year and the date of their birth, and the Questioners favorite color. This little slip can reach him by any means you like, and will be sent back a few days after you seek his answer, and he believes he can assure you, that he will have been able to satisfy you.

If a dream impresses you, by its charm or by its horror, communicate it in writing, what it sparks in your imaginations. You will be amazed how much its interpretation depicts or reassures your spirit.

Etteilla, eager to prove his science, the fun, makes sure to give you the name of the good Genius, who takes care of your conservation.[10]

And if your happiness is built on numbers which you like to put to use, Etteilla extracting from these amusing calculations the summary of the numbers of your letters, of your arrival in the big journey of life; and of your favorite color, will give you these numbers. It is not that he claims to force fortune to be subjugated to you: for when it is a matter of speaking to this beautiful Lady, Etteilla, comforter born of the unfortunate, and eager to be useful, would like to present his offerings, hat in hand, to this Goddess; and if she sometimes smiles back, he says: Alas! The true happiness of the sage is to make other people happy.

---

[10] Etteilla would not want the man, who sees himself overwhelmed by sorrows, whatever their nature, give way to despair, because, says this wise Cabalist, the good Genius, who directs all your steps, and who watches the conduct of your person, sees how little confidence you have in him, you forsake him in part, however to the contrary he would defeat the evil geniuses, which are harmful to you, if only you had the belief in the force and power, which he has over them.

ETTEILLA,

OR

THE ONLY WAY
TO DRAW THE CARDS.

=================================

READER,

I said in my first edition, and I will I say again in this second, that the amusement I am dealing with is, without doubt, the tomb of boredom, the soul in reflection, the father of advice, the amusements of society; and if you pay attention to it, you will not see any other kind of pastime, where the mind has more to strive for than in this one. It is not an amusement, in which the soul becomes angry and dejected. Nor is it, as some stupid or malicious critics want to insinuate, a black magic which gradually draws you into the abyss. Everything here just relies on combinations, simple, natural and fun, infinitely varied, depending on the arrangements of the cards brought on to the table, and from which, by their variation, show the knowledge of all the events of life, past, present and of what to come. It invites the seeker, in a pleasant way, to reflect, either, as I have just said, by showing before his eyes the evolution of the three time periods of nature; so that we can say that my Etteilla is a complete library of all that has been, is, and will be, or could even be written. It is therefore a faithful picture of human life, representing the fortuitous contests of events in which man is caught in a fisherman's net, and where a superior power forces man to fall into hell at will.

Such is this work, which I dare assure the Philosopher, the Historian, the Poet, the Novelist, the Scientist, the Mathematician himself, as well as the Father of the family, the Woman of the day, or the Woman retired, the Man of the world or the solitary, and all citizen, anyone will find it pleasant and useful; which would go a long way, if I were not in a position to give indisputable proof of it.

REMARKS.

The card upright, *Situs,* is such that we must hold it to play.

The letter R on the cards of this game, or of this book, indicates the reversal[11] of the card.

From the cards title and their assigned number is derived their primary meanings.

From their inverse[12] is derived their secondary meaning.

The draw[13] is the explanation of the entire row, which is on the table.

The counter-draw, from one row of cards to the other, and sometimes within the same row.

The set[14] is to explain several Kings, Queens, Jacks, Aces, Tens, and such.

---

[11] Translator: *Renversement.* Please note today in French one would say *inversee.*

[12] Translator: *Surnoms.*

[13] Translator: *Le Coup,* meaning the blow or the throw is the word used in the original text in French. The modern term would be *tirage.*

[14] Translator: *Ensemble.*

The joining, these are two numbers, that can join together, like the 14 and the 17.

The pairing, is to take a card on the right and place it on the one, which is on the left, placing them in parallel, two by two.

The Nil, these are cards arranged, as to not say anything.

This first explanation cannot be very clear to you, student, unless you have read my book with some patience. My fun is easy to learn, but I have to tell you in advance, that you will have some Latin, if but for you to take the trouble to read a dictionary, this is how to study my game with ease. I invite you to put the written cards on the table, as you see them in my spreads, and combine them in the following way, as I have outlined them for you.

Delectamentum jucundius quam utilius.[15]

The No. 1. ....   the Etteilla.

The No. 2. The King of **Diamonds** on his card means a Man.

Reversed, it is another Man.

The No. 3. The Queen is a Woman.

R. ...another Woman.

The No. 4. The Jack, Military.

R. ...Domestic.

The No. 5. The Ace, a Letter.

R. ...Bulletin.

The No. 6. The Ten, Gold.

R. ...Treason.

The No. 7. The Nine, Delays.

R. ...Initiative.

The No. 8. The Eight, Countryside.

R. ...Grief.

The No. 9. The Seven, Schemes.

R. ...Birth

The No. 10, 11, 12 and 15 are four Individuals.

R. *id.*

---

[15] Translator: Latin for *Delicious enjoyable rather than beneficial.*

Thoughts for the Implied Meanings.[16]

No. 1. The Etteilla representing oneself, this card must be completely blank[17].

No. 2. Someone interested in your life.

R. The same meaning.

No. 3. A Woman ... *id.*

R. ... *id.*

No. 4. Military, General, or Soldier etc.

R. Domestic, non-Artist and Craftsman.

No. 5. Letters, we'll see if it is past, present, or future.

R. Bulletin, written or received.

No. 6. Gold, the mint.

R. Treason, we will see if we are being betrayed, or if we betray.

No. 7. Delay, business, money.

R. Business, entrepreneurship, we consult the cards to find out if we will succeed.

---

[16] Translator: These are the primary meanings by title and in the reverse their secondary.

[17] Translator: *blanche.* Playing cards in the 18th century, were often printed without patterns on the backs, as in the case with the Provot playing cards used in this book. A card showing its back would thus appear to be a blank or a white card. The Etteilla card can thus be created merely by using a card flipped on its back.

No. 8. Countryside, what pertains to it.

R. Grief, as it pertains to the past or future of the draw.

No. 9. Schemes[18], if we make them, or if others make them.

R. Birth, we will see of whom, or where we were born.

Everything can only be revealed by consulting the spread.

---

[18] Translator: *Caquets.*

The no. 10. The King of **Hearts**	Blond man.
R. . *id.*	Dark-blond.
The no. 11. The Queen	Blond woman.
R. . *id.*	Dark-blonde.
The no. 12. The Jack	Blond boy.
R. . *id.*	Dark-blond.
The Ace has no number.	Mars.
R.	Extraordinary dining.
The no. 13. The Ten	City.
R.	Inheritance.
The no. 14. The Nine	Victory.
R.	Boredom.
The no. 15. The Eight	Blond daughter.
R. . *id*	Dark blonde.
The no. 16. The Seven	Thought.
R. . .	Wish.

The Ace of Hearts has no number, but indicates that the person is hardworking.

R. Extraordinary ceremonial dining at home, or away from home.
The No. 13. City, that is to say, the city where one resides.

R. Inheritance, one can inherit without having rich relatives and that, through friends, acquaintances, or by next in line.
The No. 14. Victory, on what relates to the draw or consequences of same.

R. Bored of waiting, or being boxed in, or having nothing to do.
The No. 16. Thinking of something.

R. Desire, wants, success, money, and so on.

It is necessary, Reader, to derive all the meanings, as you see, from boredom, pain of waiting, of being in the countryside, in the city, and so on.

The no.17. The King of **Spades.** Man of the robe.

R. Widowed man.

The no.18. The Queen, Widow woman.

R. Woman of the World.

The no. 19. Jack, the dispatched page.

R. Spy.

The Ace has no No.; Venus

R. Pregnancy.

The no. 20. The Ten, Sorrows.

R. Losses.

This Nine does not have a no., Ecclesiastical.

R. Saturn.

The no. 21. Eight, Sickness.

R. Religious.

The no. 22. The Seven, Expectations.

R.. Friendship.

The no's.: 23, 24, 25, 29. Like in the Hearts, different Individuals.

The No 17. Man of the robe, and all that has to do with it, not those scheming people from the Palace who have no character.

R. Widowed man. ⌠ *Or whose partners*
The No. 18. Widowed wife ⌡   *have died*

R. Woman of the world, you will see if it is present, past, or future.
The No. 19. Ambassadors, Envoys.

R. Spy, many people do it by themselves by their imprudence or by talking too much.
The Ace. Venus, the person loves pleasures. The lack of chastity is suspected, although one can be in love and be chaste too.

R. Pregnancy, we will see whose, past, present, and in the future.
 The No. 20. Grieving, for whom.

R. Losses., Money, lawsuits and the like.
The Nine. Clerical this card is the best combination in my draw: because it tramples death underfoot, as if it scorns it, having already died to the world, that is to say to the pleasures.

R. Saturn which indicates mortality of what falls on it.

The No. 21. Illnesses of mind, body, purse and so on.

    R. Religious, woman in cloister.

The No. 22. Expectations, of what presents itself.

    R. Friendship, we see with whom, or why.

The no. 23. The King of **Clover,** brown haired man.

R. *id.* Dark brown.

The no. 24. The Queen, brown haired woman.

R. *id.* Dark Brown.

The no. 25. The Jack, the Brown haired boy.

R. *id.* Dark Brown.

The no. 26. The Ace, money purse.

R. Nobility,

The no. 27. The Ten, House.

R. Lover.

The no. 28. The Nine, Effects.

R. A present.

The no. 29. The Eight, Brown haired girl.

R. Dark Brown haired girl.

The no. 30. The Seven, money.

R. Embarrassment.

Ace. Money purse; that is to say plenty of money.

R. Nobility, we'll see who.

The no. 27. House, where one resides.

R. Lover, partner.

The no. 28. Effects, such as Jewelry, furniture, clothing.

R. A Present, we will see if we receive it, or if we give it, and from whom.

The no. 30. Coined money.

R. Business embarrassment; money, occupation, children, household and so on.

You have to reflect carefully, before judging your spread.

The meanings of your numbers[19]

No. 1. Indicates nothing here.

No. 2. Loyalty.

No. 3. The Air.

No 4. Pride.

No. 5. Solitude.

No. 6. Water.

No. 7. Poverty.

No. 8. Wealth.

No. 9. The present.

No. 10. Attributes of the person.

No 11. Inconsistency,

No. 12. Generosity.

No. 13. Envy.

No. 14. Curiosity

No. 15. Flowers.

---

[19] Translator: These are the primary meanings by the assigned numbers, i.e. the 7 of Diamonds is the no. 9 and would represent the present.

2. Loyalty; either in love, in secrecy, in business, in goods, in service.

3. Air, one of the Elements, we will see if it is good for the person, I say good, in addition to normal good; because without one of the four, we would die, fire does not just spark from wood.

4. Pride, we'll see whose.

5. Solitude, we will see if we love it, or if we are forced to do so by abandoning society.

6. Water, Element.

7. Poverty, according to the person's situation.

8. Wealth, according to the person's situation.

9. The Present, the right time..

10. Observations, like buttons, sewing, small pox.

11. Inconsistency, either by whim, or by weakness depending on the issue.

12. Generosity, in rendering a service, delivering goods on time, or the opposite.

13. Envious, who is, of whom, and of what.

14. Curiosity, wanting to know everything.

15. Flowers, if we love them, or if we hate them, if we have received them as a present.

No. 16. Heart.

No. 17. Science

No, 18. Life.

No. 19. Company.

No. 20. Jealousy.

No. 21. Caution.

No. 22. Strength.

No. 23. Less.

No. 24. Talkative.

No. 25. Spirit.

No. 26. Orphan.

No 27. The future.

No. 28. Indiscretion.

No. 29. Art.

No. 30. Hatred.

No. 16. Heart, we will see if he is good, big, mediocre, bad, who he is.

No. 17. Sciences, we will see if we enjoy them, if we practice them.

No. 18. Life, we will see if good or bad.

No. 19. Company, we will see in what manner.

No. 20. Jealousy, depended on what subject, if it is well founded.

No. 21. Caution, in what way.

No. 22. Strength, spirit, love and so on.

No. 23. Less, in money, business, or prison, will be less than you expect.

No. 24. Talkative, talking too much.

No. 25. Spirit, great, strong or weak.

No. 26. Orphan, father or mother, or both.

No. 27. Future, time to come.

No. 28. Indiscretion, secrecy, vice, accommodative, dining.

No. 29. Art, Artist.

No. 30. Hatred, if one wants it, or if you want it, escaping the issue.

Meanings of numbers reversed.[20]

No. 1. has no meaning here.

No. 2. Father.

No. 3. Mother.

No. 4. Parent.

No. 5. Stepfather.

No. 6. Beginning

No. 7. Advantage.

No. 8. End.

No. 9. Good.

No. 10. Tutor.

No. 11. Mother-in-law.

No. 12. Child.

No. 13. Forced marriage.

No. 14. Impediment.

No. 15. Sister.

---

[20] Translator: In the original text in French the word is *renverses,* which can be translated as overturned or toppled. The inverse, are the secondary meanings attributed to the cards numbers, i.e. The King of Hearts is the no. 10 and would in this list be the Tutor.

The No. 2, 3, 4, 5, 10, 11, 12 and 15 are all relations, one counts as they appear and for whom they appear.

No. 6. Beginning of a trial, a case, an establishment.

No. 7. Advantage in a business, and so on.

No. 8. End, of trial, of grief.

No. 9. Good, good things to finish, to arrange, to undertake.

No. 13. Marriage forced by Parents, by state, by famine, and so on.

No. 14. Impediments in an affair; in an expectation, with a gift; I will not list all here. But you will suppose it by reflecting on it, of the good etc., one would know the meaning of it, depending where it fell; if on bad, I would say, according to the spread[21], your business is good, but will eventually turn out bad; if on the contrary the bad one fell, Well, I would say, your business is bad, but it will turn out well.

---

[21] Translator: *Le Coup du Jeu* or "the blow of the game".

No. 16 Hypocrisy.

No. 17. Weakness in courage.

No. 18. Stinginess,

No. 19. Abduction,

No. 20. Fire,

No. 21. Ambition,

No. 22. Indecision.

No. 23. Husband.

No. 24. Wife,

No. 25. Brother.

No. 26. Grudge

No. 27. The past,

No. 28. Games.

No. 29. Remoteness.

No. 30. The Land.

16. Hypocrisy, devotion pretended, or dishonesty.

17. Weakness of valor, indicates a girlish man.

18. Stinginess, money, work etc.

19. Abduction, kidnapping.

20. Fire, Element.

21. Ambition, Good, Glory, etc.

22. Indecision, not knowing which side to take, you will consult the cards.

23. Married man.

24. Married woman.

25. Brother, as with other relatives, we will see who this brother is.

26. Grudge, not willing to forgive.

27. The past, time that has gone by.

28. Game, Player, lazy man, who thinks he has all the sweets of life while playing.

29. Remoteness, we will see if it is forced, or of good will, or exile.

30. The Earth, Element.

Meanings of Joining Numbers.

No.1 and 30. Bastards.

2 and 29. Thief.

3 and 28. Extraordinary life.

4 and 27. Genealogy.

5 and 26. Bad.

6 and 25. Cession of all grief.

7 and 24. Disunity.

8 and 23. Faith.

9 and 22. Time.

10 and 21. Abuse.

11 and 20. Outrage.

12 and 19. Politics.

13 and 18. Drunkenness.

14 and 17. Unbelief.

15 and 16. Peace.

Bastard; does not mean dishonesty, but the feeling.

Thief, we'll see who, and if he has bad company.

Extraordinary life, of good or of bad depending on the draw.

Genealogy; we will see if it is good or bad.

Cession, of sorrows, of business, etc.

Disunity, friends, society, household.

Faith, promise, good or bad.

Time, we'll see what we spend it on.

Abuse, affecting what.

Outrage, effects, or words.

Political, we will see if we are good, bad, great etc.

Drunkenness, Drunkards, they want to have things their own way, they are animals who I despise.

Unbelief, this vice is even greater.

Peace, should be understood in several ways; the one who falls on Peace, will seek it and request it. Peace, after a dispute, whether one wishes Peace, and so on.

Next to the Etteilla, but on the left.

From the King of Diamonds   Gold for you.
From the Queen   Character.
From the Jack   We are waiting for you.
From the Ace   Urgent need.
From the Ten   Fall.
From the Nine   Chastity.
From the Eight   Wisdom.
From the Seven   Plenty.

From the King of Hearts   Cloister.
From the Queen   More.
From the Jack   Superstition.
From the Ace   Distrust.
From the Ten   Sincerity.
From the Nine   Despair.
From the Eight   Owed.
From Seven   Debt.

Gold for you; meaning you will have it in your
pockets.

Character, is he good, we will see who it falls on,

and we will judge whether the person is of good
or bad character, depending on the draw.

We are waiting for you, you have to see who is
waiting.

Urgent need, money, etc.

Fall, downfall. Be it big, bad, and where.

Chastity, we will see if there is.

Wisdom, in one's undertakings, in one's conduct
etc.

Plenty of business, lots of money.

Cloister, past, or future.

More, than we hope for.

Superstition; believing, for example, that my
book is supernatural, which it is not.

Distrust, of the future, of being deceived.

Sincerity, speaking the truth.

Despair, all you need is a little patience: good
and evil follow one another, even this cannot be
otherwise; nothing is perfect in man.

Dues, what we are owed.

Debts, we owe a little or a lot, depending on the
draw.

*You will put out whatever meaning, in accordance
with the necessity of things.*

In addition.

From the King of Spades	Innocent in irons.
From the Queen	Cuckold.
From the Jack	Double marriage.
From the Ace	Abandonment.
From the Ten	Inhumanity.
From the Nine	Humanity.
From the Eight	Loneliness
From the Seven	Trials.

From King of Clover	Hostility.
From Queen	Injustice.
From Jack	Flattery.
From Ace	Prison.
From Ten	Large.
From Nine	Ingratitude.
From Eight	Weakness.
From Seven	Imagination.

From the Seven, it will be observed that all these Cards, even reversed, will have the same meanings, being, as I said, next to the Etteilla.

Innocent in irons, you will need to see who is holding him back.

Cuckold, to cuckold man, P. woman, cuckold woman, libertine man.

Double marriage, we have been, we are, or we will be married a multiple of times.

Abandonment, of faith, of the good one's children.

Inhumanity, to be cruel.

Humanity, human being.

Solitude, love it or hate it.

Trial, with whom, of what; if one will win.

Hostility, does not indicate hate, it is the middle.

Injustice, if it was done to us, or by us.

Flattery, to be flattering, to speak badly in order to attract others.

Prison, a place where one loses, on entering, half of one's life, and where one has great difficulty in keeping the other together.

Big, of heart, of soul.

Ingratitude, we will see who is ungrateful.

Weakness of spirit, a good heart.

Imagination, to imagine vague and sensitive things, to come up with the idea.

Meanings of several Cards together in a spread.

4. Kings	Great honor.
4. Queens	Great talking.
4. Jacks	Contagious disease.
4. Ace	Lottery.
4. Ten	Reprisals from Justice.
4. Nine	Good Citizen.
4. Eight	Setbacks.
4. Seven	Intrigues.

3. Kings	Consultation.
3. Queens	Woman deceptions.
3. Jacks	Disputes.
3. Ace	Small Success.
3. Ten	New State.
3. Nine	Great Success.
3. Eight	Marriage.
3. Seven	Disabilities.

2. Kings	Little advice.
2. Queens	Friends.
2. Jacks	Concerns.
2. Ace	Deception.

2. Ten	Change.
2. Nine	Small money.
2. Eight	New knowledge.
2. Seven	Small news.

Great honor, relevant to the situation of the person.

Great, talked about, business negotiations and so on.

Diseases, which have cured, such as scurvy, smallpox.

Lottery, we see if we will win, or if we have put a lot into it, depending on the draw.

Results from the courts, what, of the past, in the future.

Good Citizen, will be useful to his country, in general, or in particular.

Setbacks, things which one would can expect, and which is not thought of.

Intrigue, either for good or for evil. Business affairs etc.

Consultation, business.

Woman's deception, on the side of good, love, honor etc.

Dispute, with whom. Small success, with what.

New state, what will it be.

Great Success, in what way.

Marriage, we see if it is present or in the future.

There is also another way to read Marriage; it's the Nine of Spades between a Boy and a Girl.

Disability, of body, mind, business etc.

Little advice; that is to say; council by the little mind.

Friend, present, future, Friend does not imply lover.

Concerns, of what.

Deception, how, and from whom.

Change of place, where to go, of conduct, of feeling, of house.

Small money, little.

New knowledge, small but good; it is a feeling received.

Small news, not very interesting.

Other meanings of inverted cards.

4 Kings	Sudden.
4 Queens	Bad group of women.
4 Jacks	Deprivation.
4 Ace	Dishonors.
4 Ten	Events.
4 Nine	Usury.
4 Eight	Errors.
4 Seven	Dreadful citizens.
3 Kings	Trade.
3 Queens	Gluttony.
3 Jacks	Sloth.
3 Ace	Wastefulness.
3 Ten	Lack.
3 Nine	Imprudence.
3 Eight	Show.
3 Seven	Joy.
2 Kings	Project.
2 Queens	Worker.
2 Jacks	Company.
2 Ace	Enemy.

2 Ten	Wait.
2 Nine	Profits.
2 Eight	Crossing.
2 Seven	Conduct.

Sudden business, trials at an hour you least expect.

Bad group of women or men.

Deprivation, of money, of goods, of freedom.

Dishonor, we'll see who to blame.

Event, we will see if it is good or bad.

Usury, Usurer; they will not buy my book, but will try to borrow it.

Error, in thinking, in business.

Dreadful citizen, wicked man, without money.

Trade; man of commerce, good commerce etc.

Gluttony, Greed for good or for bad.

Sloth, lukewarm man, lazy affairs, which result in nothing.

Wastefulness, indirectly resulting from corruption.

Lack, this card causes the good card on which it falls to collapse.

Imprudence, in business, in words.

Show, if there is one, go there.

Joy, gains, pleasures etc.

Project, constructive thoughts.

Workers, trades people, work.

Company, associations.

Enemy, a matter which is costly to us, is also a silent Enemy.

Waiting, languishing in the expectation of some business, money etc.

Profits, from what.

Crossings[22], in business, in enterprise.

Conduct, good or bad, and in general as with gluttony, to think that a card which appears to announce us an evil, often denotes profit for us.

This game, according to me, is very amusing: are you alone in your room; waiting for a lover for dinner, we will see if he comes; if we are trapped in a situation. I have had recourse to my game, which has prevented me more than a thousand times from giving to the devil, by those who were the authors.

---

[22] Translator: *Traverses.*

I thought I should make these reflections which will help you use the cards; so let's return to other things.

That's already 218 meanings, as you can see, in the 33 cards: Where are all my Schoolchildren who were never able to retain a quarter of it, and who in spite of me, never wanted to put it into their heads, that a card upright may not have the same meaning as one reversed?

But there is more, albeit very simple. Posing on the table is the Seven of Spades, upright[23] which indicates expectations; drop one more upright, but to the left, 32 cards one after the other, you will find 32 different means of expectations; then turn them upside down, there is another 32, similarly for the numbers, there are 128 meanings, all different, multiplied separately with each card, by repeating this same operation,

---

[23] Translator: In the original text in French the word *assiette* or plate is used to denote a card's position.

32 turns out to be 128, which make 4096 meanings in sum; but instead of having placed all of these cards to the left, place them now to the right; that's quite another change; because while your Expectation has fallen on the Lover, the Lover now falls on your Expectations, which makes a big difference; as you can see; but it is not all just Expectations, as a counter-draw, with 2 cards, with 3, with 10 etc., and with Expectations now reversed, which means Friendships, think about it, but without breaking your head, have fun. For me, its proof in hand, I find 14367 meanings in my Game, in a similar way, like me, you will find: the aspects of my schoolchildren, and of all of these little card spreads!

Let us now see how we distinguish between times, age or affairs.

It is a rule, it must be in a draw of Twelve, and when the Etteilla is drawn, you take the following number on your left, which is after it, in the upright, even if there are cards reversed between it and this first card upright, however I say; if it is not drawn, you will continue on the right, meaning, while doing the wheel; suppose, for example, that the card, drawn after the Etteilla on the left, is the number 11, you will say 13 times 11, of which you will take a quarter, which is 35 .... 9[24].

You want to know how old the husband you will marry will be; you should not say, by taking the aforementioned quarter, he will be 35 months, and 9 hours or days, but you will say, more sensibly, he will be 35 years and 9 months: if it was for a trial, you would not say, it will end in 35 years, 9 months; instead in 35 months, 2 days, 6 hours, or 35 days and 18 hours. You may say that there are trials that last 35 years, 9 months; this is not common; but to prevent them from lasting so long, do not plead.

You must therefore always take the sensible view: if you completely ignore the time in age or of the affaire, you will end up waiting quarter after quarter; remember, a thousand years and more of decisive and respectable decrees. Anyhow, if I did not tell you the numbers that can be used, you would be even less ahead. So here they are.

---

[24] Translator: 13x11=143. 143/4=35,75. 0,75x12=9.

Numbers 4, 5, 6, 7, 8, 9, 10, 11, 12, 13, 14, 15, 16 and 17 apply for women. And some more for men 18, 19, 20 and 21. All the others only count after the draw. Children do not start counting in time until they are 13 years of age; by age 68 years and 3 months, men no longer count; women only count up to 55 years and 3 months. If you want to object to my game, you would not be amused, I have made my own reflections on this topic.

It is still an observation on time, if you say 13 multiplied by 5 is 65, then a quarter, say in years, which is 16 years and 3 months; now say 13 multiplied by 6 is 78; the quarter is 19 years and 6 months; from 16 years and 3 months, to 19 years 6 months, is a space of 39 months, that you are not seeing. So you will take the number that will count, the one that will come next, to the one you have just used, still in the upright, and you will take the quarter of it, which I suppose to be the number 29; you will then say, the quarter of 29 is 7 months; because observe that these numbers, which I only use in 2s are always months; change 1 month to 30 days; for all my months are 30 days;

by 30 days this turns into 7 days and 12 hours. So you will tell the person on the number 13 multiplied by 5, as these 2 numbers followed each other as I designated them, that she is 16 years, 10 months, 7 days and 12 hours old.

I am now going to show you 4 spreads, which will introduce you to the Game, and the road you must take to have fun, and will give you on this same occasion a glimpse of the life of a Lady. I use 33 cards, Kings, Queens, Jacks, Ace, Ten, Nine, Eight, Seven, and a white card, blank on both sides[25].

For the Etteilla, I note on a blank card the no. 1, on the Ace of Diamonds the no. 5[26], on 10 of Diamonds the no. 6, on 8 of Diamonds no. 8, as well as all the others, but particularly on these to tell the upright from reverse.

For you, Reader, who wants to have fun with my Game, note on each card the numbers in a corner on the top, the cards primary meanings and

---

[25] Translator: Etteilla applies the words *blanche* and *blanc* interchangeably. Both would imply white or blank. I have here interposed both words in English into the text in order to bridge them.
[26] Translator: These numbers refer back to the numbers Etteilla has assigned to the cards. See p. 35.

secondary meanings; this will make it easier for you, until, like me, you know them by heart.

The more you feel it is somewhat difficult, the more you will do my combinations justice. However, the more you understand it, the more fun you will have. I confess to you that I, who have sometimes been tired of talking, has had a secret joy in seeing specific spreads with their explanations; and I have sometimes seen moments of enthusiasm in them; but I do not need any reflections, to know how much chance enters into the predictions they seem to make; and in their accuracy, and that of all the truths in the drawing of these cards, one should not lose sight of, the least, that there is nothing on which one should rely less than, on the events that they announce.

My method of explaining will seem bizarre to you; but the quintessence in what I derive from all my meanings, makes for a continuous game, as you will see, while you reflect, *Note*.

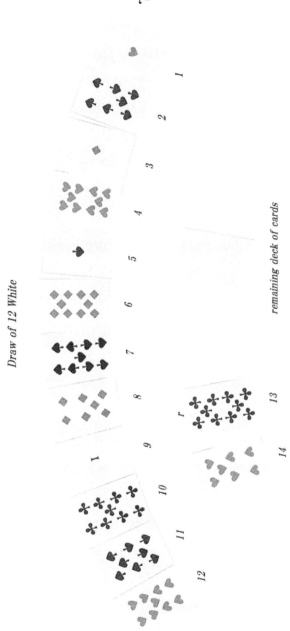

Draw of 12 White

remaining deck of cards

*Cards shown are the reproduced Provot from the 1790s. With kind
permission from the JC Flornoy Estate. www.tarot-history.com*

I have drawn these cards for people far away, in letter correspondences, them sending me the illustrations of the spreads. Regardless, shuffle your cards well from top to bottom without looking at them, and cut with any hand you like, as this reservation is made only by bad card slingers[27], only the thought has an impact on this Game: just as we can cut for a person absent.

After cutting, you will arrange 12 cards as they appear one by one, side by side, as you see them illustrated; turn over the thirteenth, and put it below and one at the heel on the table, which will be the fourteenth, such as you see in this spread. I now return to this Lady, that I told you about; observe that the first card is across you, on your right, and the last one in the end that follows. You can see the cards are numbered below, this number is only there for me to better explain myself, or make it more clear.

Here then is the shape of the first draw, which is called the Draw of Twelve, has to be, because the two at the heel, although they speak their

---

[27] Translator: *Tireurs de cartes.* Etteilla will later change his view on this...

meanings, do not count in the numbering, I will come back to this.

This Lady sent for me, and after the formal pleasantries, I took my Etteilla, which I shuffled well from top to bottom, and after she had made the cut, I drew the 12 cards without the court cards[28]; I did not fail to tell her, that she was a woman and not a man, as she then was disguised in order to test me. Observe that this similar draw of 12 without any courts, neither the 9 of Clover nor that of Hearts, imply this meaning: If the 8 of Spades was the only inversed card in this draw of White, it would indicate a disguised Nun; if the 9 of Spades upright appeared alone, it would indicate a clergyman in disguise.[29]

If both appeared in the same draw, signifying a person, this would resolve the meaning of the disguise, and that would explain the draw; Lover[30] is also a person as well as Stepfather[31], whether

---

[28] Translator: *Figures.*

[29] Translator: The 8 of Spades Reverse implies Religion and the 9 of Spades implies Ecclesiastical. See p. 40.

[30] Translator: Presumably Card no. 27 the Ten of Clover Reversed. See p. 43.

[31] Translator: Presumably Card no. 5. Ace of Diamonds, reverse-numbered meaning. See p. 49.

the Etteilla appears or does not appear, does not disrupt anything, it is by itself a blank card: I therefore say when this card appears, the blank card would announce a disguise, nothing more[32]; as found when immediately redoing this draw of 12, which I do, I combine, examine, and after noticing all the aspects of my spread, I retain what is the most interesting, in order to be able to explain it; So I can return to the path of truth, that all seekers must follow in order to be able to read the cards quickly and easily.

Whether or not the Etteilla appears in this draw, it is always necessary to notice what the first person to arrive is, to attribute to it, the person for whom one reads[33], admitting that there is the possibility that the 1 may mean such.

Suppose; I drew cards for a woman; the first court card which appears in the draw is the King of Hearts, I will not say to the woman; here you are in King of Hearts, that would be ridiculous;

---

[32] Translator: To the confused reader, yes, Etteilla is explaining how he was not able to see the type of disguise in his spread, and then proceeds to explain how one could, without providing a real-life example.

[33] Translator: In the original text the word used is *opere* or operate.

but if the woman for whom I am reading is dark-haired, and the Queen of Clover is not there, I go to the Etteilla; if it's there, I always explain my moves to the Questioner, and I just say that she is neither in the Etteilla, in the draw nor in a court defining her color; there is everything to believe, and to tell her that she is not in the center of her affairs, perhaps because she has great follies, and in this, we arrive at the most sensitive aspect of the Game.

But back to this spread of Twelve, which must always be the first drawn, remember that when there is no person in the initial draw, one immediately expects to see the Etteilla commanding the following card.

The Etteilla let's us know, we start to say when we speak directly to the person, you are just 26 years old. If the person was absent, I would have said: you made me read on a woman with inclination; she is 26 years old. Since it should be noted that if a client asks us to draw her the cards, without telling us for whom, we must not, like all these little card slingers, ask her; But rather take the Etteilla and beat them to it.

Shuffle well top to bottom, cut for the Questioner, and draw twelve cards, pay attention to the first person which appears in the draw, all the while taking the sensitive approach; that is, if a man asks us this question, and the Lover appears first, we must answer him in the affirmative: It is for your Lover, that you want these cards to be drawn; and then you will see his color in the first figure of the female sex, which appears, while observing to be careful whether this female is single, married or widow, or even in cloister, and you tell him forthright, her family, status, her condition and her age, to which I will come back to, taking into account that it is this woman, who is the subject of the spread.

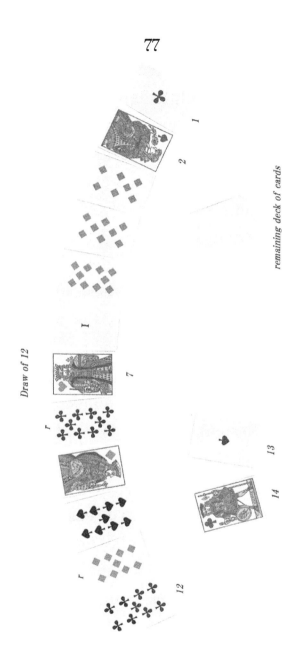

Cards shown are the reproduced Provot from the 1790s. With kind permission from the JC Flornoy Estate. www.tarot-history.com

The spread of Twelve being therefore on the table, we see if the Etteilla is there, because note that if it is not, one cannot count the age of the persons, nor the time in affairs; but when it is, it counts as thirteen, and indicates thirteen times 27^{34}; please observe that we must not say thirteen times the number of the card[35] which is next to Etteilla, on his right, and which, therefore, is to the left of the reader. We therefore begin, as I said, to count thirteen times the number of the second card; and thirteen times twenty-seven you cannot count, for two reasons: the first is that the number twenty-seven only counts in months; see page 68. Second reason, is that the card is reversed, and that for the numbers to count, the card must be in a upright position. Thirteen times two[36] does not count, for two reasons: the first is that the number only counts for months and are too low to be years; the second is that the card is reversed. Thirteen times nothing, the cards from

---

[34] Translator: Card no. 27 is the Ten of Clover, here in the reverse. See p. 43.

[35] Translator: The card left of the Etteilla. The King of Hearts.

[36] Translator: Card no. 2 would be the King of Diamonds. Here reversed. See p. 35.

the Nine of Spades, do not count. Thirteen times twenty-six[37] does not count either. Thirteen times eighteen[38] does not count for women. Thirteen times nine[39] is reversed. Thirteen times eight[40], this number being in the upright position, and moreover in the row of those which count for years, it is necessary to use it, so as to say; thirteen times 8 is 104.

The quarter is twenty-six, we must now see if there are any cards, that have numbers implying months that can increase the age from twenty-six. The client must make sure whether this is the case; assuming, she is reading this composition[41], while the cards of her spread are placed in front of her, as they appear in the illustration; but if, suppose, the 23[42] or other had come upright[43], appearing before the no. 8. not passing the Etteilla, we would have said simply, a quarter of the 23-months is 5

---

[37] Translator: Card no. 26 is the Ace of Clover, reversed. See p. 43.

[38] Translator: Card no. 18 the Queen of Spades, reversed. See p. 40.

[39] Translator: Card no. 9 the Seven of Diamonds. Here reversed.

[40] Translator: Card no. 8 would be the Eight of Diamonds. See p. 35.

[41] Translator: *Traite*.

[42] Translator: Card no. 23 is the King of Clover. See p. 43.

[43] Translator: *Bien dispose sur son assiette*, i.e. well-positioned or upright.

months, 22 days, 12 hours, and we would have added that to this woman's 26th birthday.[44]

But a true Seeker would ask us, to see how long his trials will last and such. Without making him too acrimonious except by my amusement, it will be dispatched more promptly, and it will cost him much less; I will show him, when they will be completed. To succeed, we will therefore take the same route as for the age; and instead of counting years, we will count months, and then months over to days; always keeping in mind the calculations in years, in case of an event; therefore it should be noted, that it is always necessary to take the most responsible time perspective. Some jokers have assured me that women cannot count up to 55; and some icy cabalists, have assured me, that men count up to 72, a period of 36 up and down. I do not oppose

---

[44] Etteilla believed it necessary to put here by note, that to understand the manner of drawing the cards, and even all of their compositions, it is absolutely necessary for the seeker to present his spreads such as they are described in the illustrations, as it is derived from it. To say, otherwise one would be certain to advance towards not being able to hear it. All reasonable men readily understand the difficulties of operating from theory alone, especially in a genre which has not been dealt with by any other.

these two sentiments; but I maintain none the less that my rule is good for ages and time periods, when one knows how to calculate them well.

Let's return; because in order to respond to criticisms, and to trace all that would be necessary to complete this work entirely, we would need at least another folio, the price of which would certainly terrify more than encourage the learning of the manner of drawing the cards. What will our icy men say. So, I study the first aspect of this draw of Twelve, which is; I am working for woman with a title; she has an inclination that degrades her quality; she was born in the countryside; near a river; and her father had her put in a cloister; and he died of sorrow; that she has a Lover; and that she was, as I said, 26 years old when she consulted me. Let us justify this by studying the spread.

The Questioner visible to our eyes, that is to say, making it obvious, is in a connection with a parliamentarian, an inclined woman, and their conversation is along that of the nobility; but as the first figure appearing in the draw designates the Questioner, we cut short, and say that the

Queen of Spades[45] denotes what she is; the Ace of Clover[46], who has come to her side, says that she is of good nobility. For its sex, we cannot see; because in this draw there is no other feminine card with sex. To know if she is married or not, we can't say that right now either, not from this.

Nobility, we go find the Questioner, who is a woman of inclination; she was born in the country, around water, which I say is a river; because I only see good in this spread. If there was good and bad, I would say by the sea, or above, depending on the reading, whether a counter-draw; if there were only bad ones, I would say water hole, well. Gold[47] will find Etteilla, and this gold is from the countryside; she will however give it to her Lover, who is a fair-haired man[48]: another man will speak to her about a death; if he himself does not commit the follies, that leads it

[45] Translator: The Queen of Spades is card no. 18 and denotes, in reverse, a woman of the world. See p. 40.

[46] Translator: The Ace of Clover is Nobility in the Reverse. See 43.

[47] The King of Diamonds to the left of the Etteilla Gold. See p. 55.

[48] Translator: The King of Hearts implies blond. The Lover is the Ten of Clover reversed. Presumably the Eight of Diamonds implies the countryside. See p. 35, 38 and 43.

there, and a notion of a present is with the Questioner; but she will not accept it.

At the bottom, the meaning of the numbers are implied. She has a grudge[49] against someone who does not do her good, or at least to someone other than herself. Wealth falls into water[50]; if there here was a meaning relating to commerce, I could, according to the arrangement of the cards, say that her property will perish by water; but I won't; I am only going to say that from being rich, she will go to famine or mediocrity; but it does not last; for her Lover, falling back on water, knows how to build wealth. Etteilla comes across an observation; the past falls on her father, and the father on Saturn[51]; I would say he is dead. She will have an advantage in this spread. Both cards at the heel indicate she is pregnant with a boy, he will be brown-haired.[52]

---

[49] Translator: Presumably the grudge is implied by the Ace of Clover in Reverse, no. 26. secondary meaning by number. See p. 43 and 51.

[50] Translator: Presumably the Ten of Diamonds, no. 6, represents the water. See p. 45.

[51] Translator: The King of Diamonds is card no. 2 in reverse, father, in position 9, with Nine of Spades in the reverse, implying Saturn. See p. 40 and 49.

[52] Translator: The pregnancy is indicated by the Ace Reversed and the brown-haired boy by the Jack of Clover. See p. 40 and 43.

I feel that those who have learned the lessons from me will say that I pass. I have explained the reasoning.

The Etteilla next to the King of Hearts, means cloister; but being in the past, indicates that it is related to her Lover and such, and even the father has become poorer during those times. Let's study them together; there are only three Nines that count; for the two Kings are positioned differently, therefore the three Nines reversed indicate recklessness[53]; we must summarize the spread, we will see that this imprudence is related to him.

Pair up your cards two by two, and at the same time pay attention to joining numbers; but in this draw, there are none: the Ace of Clover, nobility; goes on the Nine of Clover, and as mentioned with this spread, a present she will not accept, that will cause her resentment. The numbers 26 and 28[54] do not count: because they add up to 31 just with the two cards[55]. The other

---

[53] Translator: 3 Nines inverted, Imprudence. See p. 62.
[54] Translator: Card no. 26 and 28 would be the Ace of Clover and the Nine of Clover. See p. 43.
[55] Translator: Card meanings stop at 30.

cards; a gallant woman, but no longer her, but, as
we have seen, at the opening of the draw, one of
the acquaintances, falls into poverty, and the
Questioner will be slow in securing money; 18 and
7 do not count[56]. Next, birth, indicates nothing[57];
mortality may be favorable here; countryside falls
on the father, he as mentioned is dead and this
occurred in the countryside[58]; a man gives wealth
to the Questioner: wealth that she use to have.
Lover does not last the same with wealth.
Remaining is the Questioner represented by
Etteilla and the man next to it. This announces
something; we will see in another spread as well
as study this person, which we cannot do from
this. In the two cards at the heel I do not see
anything in either set of cards, nor an encounter
of numbers. This spread is done, I may have left
something out, by combining it well, one could
still find some small aspects, like me seeing this

---

[56] Translator: The no. 7 and the no. 18 would be the Nine of Diamonds
and the Queen of Spades, both reversed.
[57] Translator: The Nine of Spades Reversed is Saturn and the Seven
of Diamonds indicates a birth. Presumably this implies miscarriage?
[58] Translator: The coupling between the King of Diamonds and the
Eight of Diamonds.

woman from the countryside, who is false[59], however I do not see anything, that catches my interest.

If you read a spread, without putting this same spread on your table, and read it as quickly as you would read a story, you would find in the end that you have wasted your time. This book demands to be read slowly, and to be reflected upon; and if you say you can't hear, it's because you're going ten times too fast.

---

[59] Translator: Presumably Etteilla is thinking of the Ace of Clover representing grudge, the Queen of Spades in reverse and the 2 Aces in Reverse implying enemy. See p. 62.

Let's move on to the second spread: we draw 27 cards and we put them down 9 to 9, as you can see; the last six, that which we renounce, representing things in life we discard.

On to the meanings of Kings, Queens etc. and the sets, the pairing of numbers, two by two.

You must only examine them in each row of the 9s, and not as 27 collectively; but that is not all, unlike the spread of 12, we lay the first arrival following the cut at position 1, the second at position 19, the third at position 10, and so we resume until we reach 27 following this path: please follow me from point to point.

Let's see, let's explain this spread; but you must remember that it is necessary, first of all, to combine it, if the twenty-seven cards is not a particularly interesting draw, which is essential; supposing there is nothing to see. I will come back to this. The Jack of Hearts falls on the Jack of Diamonds, which denotes a dark-blond boy, a domestic servant; no. 12 denotes a child, falling on 4, which indicates a parent; I therefore say that it is a child, a man, one of your relatives, who acts in a domestic way: but I see three Aces reversed and two Jacks reversed just prior. This looks quite interesting.

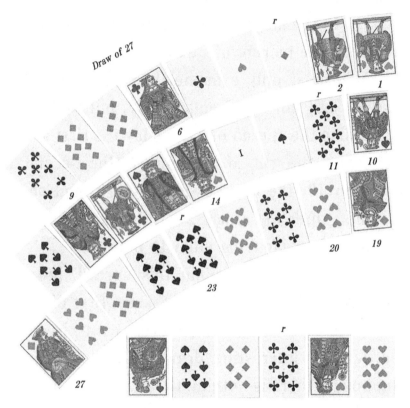

The heel of the spread amounts to nothing and is explained thus.

Cards shown are the reproduced Provot from the 1790s. With kind permission from the JC Flornoy Estate. www.tarot-history.com

In reflection, these two Jacks indicate company; the three Aces wastefulness[60]; consequently I say that you are in the company of waste, which makes me suspect that you are not married; this is not a great enough proof, however. Moving on: Extraordinary dining invite[61]: You want to know more, combine these nine cards, and you will see that this invitation will be brought to you by a dark-blond haired servant and that this extraordinary dining will take place with a dark-haired woman, on whom the dining falls: Stepfather falls on nobility[62], because the dining counts in this first draw, I would say that you have a father-in-law, consequently that your father is dead; you can see that it is your father-in-law who went to seek nobility, resulting in him securing it; because you gain nobility without you having to look for it. Now I can suppose that it is not nobility, will wait for the spread to confirm more.

---

[60] Translator: The 3 Aces reversed imply wastefulness. See p. 62.

[61] Translator: The extraordinary dining is implied by Ace of Hearts Reversed. See p. 39.

[62] Translator: The Stepfather is implied by card position 5, Nobility by Ace of Clover Reversed. See page 49 and 43.

No. 26, grudge, falling on a dark-haired woman, she's a woman you blame, reports of gossip made about the countryside[63]; no. 8 wealth falls on delay, you will be rich late in life, but you will be, because this delay falls on money; No. 7 falls on 30, poverty in resentment; poverty will make you hate; I say, that it is you who would hate someone pertaining to this poverty; which would not be the case if opposite, the no. 30 fell on 7; two Jacks, Company[64]; three Aces, wastefulness; like I said in the beginning of my draw; I don't see any joining numbers; pairing up these nine cards; the Jack of Hearts and the 7 of Clover, a blond-haired man who falls on hate; his no. 12 Jack, one of your children who falls on money, a servant who falls on poverty; he is in your spread, so he has something to do with you, is known to you and so on. His no. 4, one of your relatives, who is late in talking with you, or about his business, a letter falling on wealth, which you

---

[63] Translator: The Ace is the no. 26 in the Reverse implying grudge, the Queen of Clover dark hair, the Nines upright, Schemes, the Eight of Diamonds the countryside, 2 Jacks Concern and 2 Aces Deception. See p. 35, 43 and 59.

[64] Translator: Two Jacks Reversed implies Company. See p. 62.

send. No. 5 your father-in-law, who is in the countryside, Extraordinary dining falling on chatter. It is the dining, that we have already studied, where words will be required; a woman one of your acquaintances, falling on nobility, grudge on to renouncement.

Pertaining to every card spread in general; They are explained as I have already said, noting the most interesting aspects, which is not to say that one leaps to discard all that is not seen in the spread, of what is of interests to us. One observes and returns to it afterwards, because such things which may seem to not exist, could, indeed, if it did, could in fact be very interesting to us. You see that in this draw of nine, I explained the two Jacks and three Aces, without waiting for the end, as I did in my first spread, since my reflections on the nine cards, I note these five sensitive things as the interesting aspects.

Let us return to the second row: I combine my draw, I see an explanation in the first card, I begin to explain them; a Spy falling on a Lover; Lover falls on Venus; Venus[65] on the Etteilla, which is

---

[65] Translator: The Ace of Spades in the upright is Venus. See p. 40.

you; the Etteilla next to the King of Hearts, which indicates cloister, and by the number 10, Guardian[66] next to a man of the robe[67], a brother, an ensuing husband who falls on illness; I come back to the first one, I see an abduction in the past, brushing Venus and falls on you.

This is how I explain this row, meaning, how I set it in order. You were abducted in the past with the love from your husband, who was sick; a spy will come to take you from your lover while you enjoy the pleasures[68], and will lock you up; and four people, including your husband, your brother, your tutor and a man of the robe, consult each other for your entrapment. I see no hindrance or lack; I say therefore, that you are married, that you have been taken away, and that you will be closed off to this topic, because you are not in it now, besides the past is understood

---

[66] Translator: The King of Hearts is no. 10 and the number in reverse implies a tutor. See p. 49.

[67] Translator: This implies a man of distinction in 18th century France.

[68] Translator: Presumably the Jack of Spades no. 19, reversed implying the Spy and abduction, the Ten of Clover the Lover and the Ace of Spades, the pleasures. Sickness the Eight of Spades. The King of Clover in reverse, the husband. The King of Hearts next to the Etteilla, cloister. See p. 40, 43 51 and 55.

only for the opportunities it creates. We must now read out all the meanings of the cards, which have not spoken, and leave the meanings that have spoken: Dark-brown from your acquaintances falls on science, a boy and a dark haired man, who talk to you with caution. Here are the sets; 2 Jacks, company; 2 Kings, a project; there are no joining numbers in any of these nine cards: now pair your cards: Spy falls on caution, this spy who will remove you, will be careful; number 19[69], removal due to illness; double meaning as in a cloister or prison[70], an event you are going to expect; lover falling on husband, I would say, that your lover knows your husband. The past, a dark-brown haired man, a man you no longer meet with. Venus falling on your brother, I say that your brother seeks pleasures, and not the pleasures him; you fall on science, a man of the robe falls on tutor; the situation between these two are reported to you; a fair-haired man whom you renounced; in the third row a woman, then a blond girl, these

---

[69] Translator: The Page of Spades reversed is the no. 19. See p. 40.
[70] Translator: The King of Hearts to the left of the Etteilla would imply Cloister and the Ace to the right prison. See p. 55 and 57.

are two people you know: the number 3 is your mother; number 15, comes with flowers, lost legacy; indiscretion in your forced marriage by you; since there are no other court cards. Clergyman between fire and water, discord between you and a clergyman[71]. Gold on your mind; Hearts for a man, loyalty ends. Let's see the big picture: 2 Tens, you wait, for what? let us follow, 15 and 16, which are the joining numbers, peace probable for you, as you return home, or articulating it better, the peace you plan to make with your mother and your family, following the meanings implied by your cards. Now you, according to the rules, take them in your hand one by one and assign a meaning to them; a woman who is faithful to you, your mother who speaks to a man, blonde girl in your Heart, flowers on your mind; you love them very much, or hate them very much; but I cannot tell which of the two, not seeing it now; effects that fall, or are on water for you; fruitful indiscretion, inheritance from a

---

[71] Translator: The Nine of Spades implies something ecclesiastical. See p. 40.

clergyman; a lost forced marriage, passion waning, this element is moving away from you.

Let's examine the heel, you destroy success, its number 14[72]. I am curious to see if you will have a Mother-in-law. You renounce a dark-blonde woman, you are estranged; meaning, that you will move closer to home; you renounce a dark-brown haired woman, the cause of your birth[73], friendship, indecision, meanness, and a woman of the world, So, there you have it, your draw of 27 completed.

---

[72] Translator: The Nine of Hearts is no. 14 and implies victory. See p. 38.

[73] Translator: The heel represents what is discarded. The Queen Reversed would imply a dark-brown haired woman, the Seven of Spades trials and the Nine Reversed implies birth. See p. 35, 40.

Let's move on to the third draw, which is the Etteilla's Draw; it is done in two ways, although it is presented the same.

Here is the path that must be followed, the first way it can be explained: after having placed the cards on the table, as you see them, we combine the whole spread, and we announce what it says as with the numbers two-by-two, meaning from one card onto the other, in each row; then the sets in the 4 rows, proceeding with 4 Kings upright, 3 Tens inverted, and so on.

In summary we must look at everything that speaks out to us in the whole of the spread, with the exception, as said, with joining numbers, which is only read into in the 4 rows one at the time. When everything is well explained and there is nothing more to see, we begin with the Ace of Clover, and we proceed thus:

1

33

Tracing here the following steps, and speaking to, Etteilla, Ace, King, Queen, Jack, Ten, Nine, Eight and Seven, Etteilla, King, and so on.

If the Etteilla appears in the draw, we just continue as if it had not, and as the cards fall you will name them, you put them down into the table in this way;

The first goes to A, the second to B; and so the same for the others: when you have finished, you will pick up the rest of the cards, you will shuffle them, cut them, and you will look at two cards, the one on the heel, and the other below, which you will explain, as well as all the cards as they come, like in the draw of Twelve.

But let's move on to Etteilla's Draw to this woman. In this way, we place these cards one by one, like for the others, as I have just explained; then we combine the whole spread, starting from one end finishing in the other, the 8 across, and the 4 vertically. If these 33's were a good draw they would be explained without any interruption like in the subject of a great affair, its beginning, its ups, downs, and conclusion, and you would explain them right away, and trace your steps; it is necessary for all the cards to speak one by one, either by primary meaning, by secondary meaning, or by their consequence and so on. I repeat therefore, that before starting this draw, it is necessary, like with the others, to shuffle well, and afterwards, to follow this path. Let's start with the first eight; if I encounter a meaning of particular note, but refrain from explaining it; I will get back to it soon after; that's the way to do it, I will say what strikes me the most, every time.

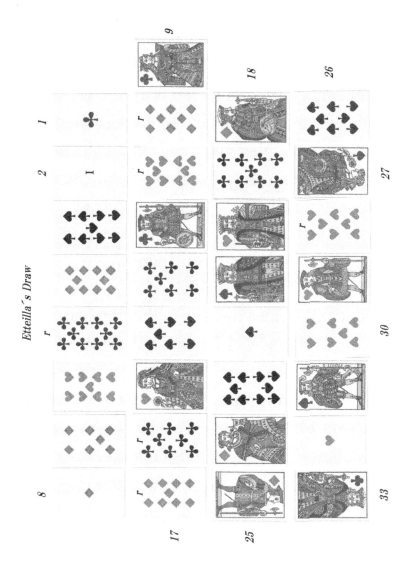

Cards shown are the reproduced Provot from the 1790s. With kind permission from the JC Flornoy Estate. www.tarot-history.com

The number 26 and the 5, bad[74], falling on the
Etteilla, the Etteilla on Saturn, Saturn on Water,
Water on Lover, Lover on Impediments,
Impediments on Good; it only takes a little
thinking to explain this move. I mentioned above
Water, accompanied by good and bad, meaning
sea; I see you, your lover and you, fall on bad
cards; I see after an obstacle falling on Good; I
say that you and your lover almost perished at
sea, consequently that you therefore traveled by
sea. If Saturn[75] would not have been there, if bad
had not fallen on you, I would have simply said,
that you had traveled by sea, but what makes me
say otherwise, is that the past is in this spread;
but let's resume; money purse falling on you, that
is to say, that money will come to you, without
you looking for it: Orphan falling on Saturn, Gold
on Lover, Water in the past. I explained that;
Boredom on birth; impediments with a letter,
loneliness for a dark-haired woman, gossip that
will cause sorrow; sin falls on heritage, there is a

---

[74] Translator: The 26 and 5 are numbers attributed to the Ace, here as
joining numbers 26+5 implying something bad. See p. 53.

[75] Translator: Saturn is represented with the Nine of Spades in
Reverse. See p. 40.

two-way understanding; but the most responsive results of this woman's schemes is, she will inherit before long; forced marriage for brown haired boy; spirit and money on expectation; with a change of mind you will have the money you hope for; hatred by force but not defined, by whom? From or towards a blonde woman; inconstancy with a dark-brown; removal from business; advantage over a man you will have; loyalty; if you consider it. You will see that I have against our rule, followed a different path; but I was constrained here. I stopped at loyalty, which does not seem to me to have much to do with the present, and I resumed at present with a blond man; you will go for it; play with a remarkable man; man of the robe falling for you on Venus[76]; science on sorrow; Venus between these two cards give cause for reflection, from where will come this science and these tears? You will still mind again that I am deviating from our path; jealousy on woman, I should say on air; but woman would

---

[76] Translator: Loyalty is implied by the King of Diamonds, who also carries the no. 2. Blond man would be the King of Hearts, brushing the King of Spades, man of the robe, of distinction and with the Ace representing Venus. See p. 35, 40 and 45.

not be explained; for it must then follow; your jealousy will therefore fall on a woman; will she be a brunette or a blonde? Follow the spread and see what first color we will see in a woman, or a girl; it is the Eight of Hearts, she will be blonde. Let's come back; air; I stop, because it does not mean anything; having fallen on home, I thus take up the rule in the first explanation, and I say; Sick servant, prudent parents, woman of the world over blond-haired, grudge on sister, blond boy over desire, generous through hypocrisy, sent to business, company of a man, husband remains; Etteilla next to the 9 of Spades, you are human.

Let us study the joining numbers, your no. 26 and 5; we have explained this, by 24 and 7, disunity; 28 and 3, an extraordinary life. In all of the spreads, I only see these three joining numbers.[77] Now let's take a look at the several cards.

Three Kings, you will consult one another; three Queens, you will be deceived by women;

---

[77] Translator: Presumably the Queen of Diamonds brushing the Nine of Diamonds implies the conflict between 3 and 28. Likewise the Queen of Hearts brushing the Seven of Diamonds creates the 24 and 7 condition.

three Jacks, arguments; 4 Aces, Lottery: it would be necessary to study if good or bad; but bad was there at the beginning, that is why you will wait for a more favorable moment to put this forward; two Tens, change; two additional Tens, waiting; four nines, usury. I do not see currently that this woman is a usurer, but it begins to let me know that she has potential for it; three Eights, show; two Sevens, small news; two more Sevens, conduct. Now remove the Etteilla from the spread, and put the Queen of Clover in its place: pair up your cards.

Money purse on prudence, you will receive money which you will spend with prudence; sick orphan, constant sorrow, sorrows that will last; end for a man; stingy brown-haired woman; gossip about a women of the world; inheritance on games, you will play away your inheritance; forced marriage by the present, Saturn on sister, brown-haired boy, remarkable in person, spirit on fair-haired man; gold coming generously, water on fair-haired boy, money on science; hate falling on a man of the robe, hypocritical Lover; past falls on desire, expectations on Venus; boredom on company, impediments in dispatch, jealous blonde woman, instability that will make you cry, birth on labor, brunette on air, estrangement from a woman, letter from your husband; solitude on man, venture on parents, one undertakes yet again, if one wants, the eight across in the same way; but I do not see anything more interesting in the story of this woman other than an inheritance in the distance; faithful servant, air in the present, jealous blond man, remarks which will come from these tears, illness for her husband, toil in his condition.

I told you that when some meaning say things that are of little interest to you, we must pass them by; i.e. if I were to tell you that the Grand Turk is the victor or the vanquisher of the Grand Mogul. Let's move on to the Wheel of Fortune: this is how it is done.

Special care must be taken, not to misinterpret the meanings of the Wheel when it is laid out. The main thing to remember is that the 8 of Clover, the 8 of Diamonds and the Ace of Spades, as they are placed, are in the upright, that the King of Clover, the Jack of Spades, the 9 of Clover are reversed, looking to the others, this can easily be seen by turning the Wheel upside down, in the top bar the King of Hearts is reversed and the 7 of Hearts is upright.

First of all we draw out the Etteilla, and we place it in the middle; after the cards have been shuffled well, always remember to do this head to tail, shuffle, and then cut.

We put down column A, then column B, starting both from below; then the wheel is put down, starting with the Queen of Diamonds; and lastly, we put out the top bar starting with the

Nine of Diamonds. Column A is the past; column B is the future; the top bar is the present; the first 4 cards on the wheel represent the past, the last four as in column B, and the 5 in the middle of the wheel as with the top bar.

The Wheel of Fortune Draw

Cards shown are the reproduced Provot from the 1790s. With kind permission from the JC Flornoy Estate. www.tarot-history.com

Now say; the Etteilla next to the Queen of Diamonds, means character. Combine this meaning with card no. 9, which implies good, and tell the Questioner: In the past you were of good character. Proceed in this way with the following cards, two by two.

The Etteilla, next to the Eight of Clover, joins with the no. 25 implying that in the past, the Questioner was not strong enough in her head, that she had weaknesses; she judged badly her strength then; she believed that she was strong enough; but she gave in, either by traps of treason or of love etc., but since these are feelings towards others, we say of love[78]. Next to the Seven of Clover, she was in the past careless of the future, not concerned with it. But let's continue with the past, before addressing the future. Together in the eight cards, we find two upright Queens and two Sevens, which is that of Spades and that of Clover: we say therefore, that in the past, a friend gave her news, but not so big that

---

[78] Translator: Card no. 25 is the Jack of Clover, a boy, but the number also implies the Spirit and other people, the Eight of Clover, a girl. See p. 43, 47 and 58.

she was expecting it; for there is only small news here. Now, pair up your cards two by two, the Queen of Diamonds and the Seven of Diamonds: a woman, was good to her, and she was born in the air; that is to say, high noon: I say that, thinking the first stroke of twelve. No. 3 and 9 do not count, so put these cards aside. Pair up the other two: a dark-haired girl dominating her mind; a dark-haired boy working as an artist, with regard to the Questioner, 29 and 25 do not count. A dark-haired woman had power over her; the Questioner had hopes, spoke up too much; 22 and 24 do not count. She made a present in the past, which presently will be spoken of or will be returned to her in future; 27 and 28 do not count[79].

Here the past has been explained, it is now necessary to address the future, while following the same principle. The Etteilla next to Ace of Clover; let us say straight away, that she will go to prison, compromised somehow in the mortality of someone: it is necessary to consult the eight card drawn, and the Seeker will verify the events

---

[79] Translator: Regarding joining numbers see p. 53.

that I have traced, and will recognize the identity of the main person in my work.

Next to the Jack of Spades, double marriage, and a child; next to the Nine of Diamonds, she will act wisely towards the envious; next to the Ace of Hearts, she will be suspicious and greedy.

The Sets here are two Jacks, which are reversed, and two Aces in the upright; they imply, that in the future, a community will be deceived. Now pair up your cards two by two; money purse will be on hold; death will be unusual around an orphan; no. 26 does not count. By following the other cards, you will spy on one of your children; a dark-blond boy will take something away from you; 19 and 12 does count, you will be political. The countryside will be envious; in the city you will become rich; 8 and 13 do not count; woman of the world says nothing; great occupation will lead you to greed. No.18 does not count. Let's look at the present.

The Etteilla next to the Seven of Clover, you think you are poorer than you actually are; next to the Ace of Diamonds, you urgently need a Guardian: next to the Ace of Spades, you

surrender yourself completely: next to the Eight
of Spades, you do not see your parents: next to
the King of Clover, you have conflicts with water.
The sets, two Kings, two Seven, you have a
project, and you are going to receive news from
it. Pair up your cards; a delay and you will hate
someone; you have money, but you are going to
leave empty handed; 7 and 30 do not count. A
dark-blond man talks about you with your father-
in-law, you are going to send a letter to a
Guardian. 10 and 5 do not count. Love is in your
heart, your mind is not in support; 16 does not
count. A Servant will be careful; illness for one of
your relatives; 21 and 4 do not count. It says here
that you will send gold to your husband, this is in
contrast; but without completely cancelling this
prognostication, I would say, that you will speak
to him about gold. A dark-brown man falls on the
water, which implies you won't see him anymore.
This draw is fairly complicated, but nothing can
be in full detail, that is not possible.

III

Fan Draw

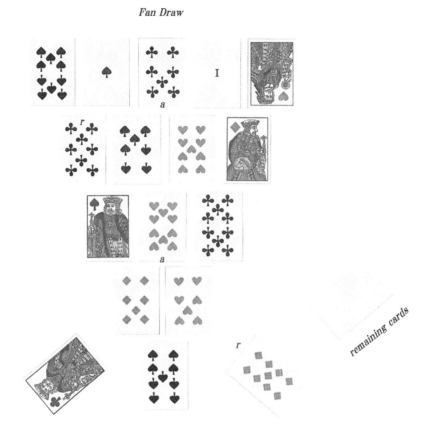

Cards shown are the reproduced Provot from the 1790s. With kind permission from the JC Flornoy Estate. www.tarot-history.com

Let us now explore the shape of the fan, or rather the great thoughts of the Heart. In explaining it you will find meanings related to the continuation of the life of our lady. This spread is explained like all the others. Cards which come in the middle, like those marked with **a** are nullified, and are explained as thus. It is not necessary to go back. This thought or fan is very easy; combine the whole of the spread, and see if you can explain it as you go along; number 11 and number 20, Outrage for you; embarrassment on Venus; 2 and 29 by a thief; tears for a man; two 8s, crossings; loyal on bored; impediments by religion; no. 27 the future; two 10s, Change; two 7s, Conduct; Saturn nullified. The entire draw, as you can see in what follows, must not have a stop, included are the two supports below: It says in short; in future you will be insulted by love, from bandits[80]; you will make up your mind and change your behavior. This will however not take place; the one who engages in the business of offending you, will be a dark-brown haired man; advantage to your husband. There is still a lot to talk about. Afterwards we will study where and in what time.

---

[80] Translator: Presumably Etteilla's conclusion here, that this woman would be insulted or perhaps violated by bandits *Brigands* traces back to several combinations; joining no. 11-20 Outrage, 2-29 Thief, Sets 2x7 Conduct, 2x9 Profits, 2x8 Crossings, 3x9R Imprudence, cards 9 of Spades R Saturn, 10 of Spades R Losses, Ace Venus lack of chastity and pleasures, King of Spades Innocent in irons etc. See p. 40, 53, 57, 62 and 63.

Here is the draw of 15, and how it is done: we shuffle[81], we cut, and now we think of three cards; I am supposing the 7 of Clover upright, Money; the 10 of Clover reversed, Lover; the third, thinking a Trial, the Etteilla next to the 7 of Spades. We draw these cards out of the pile, we put them on the table; the 7 of Clover in the first row; the 10 of Clover in the second, meaning in their starting positions; the Etteilla next to the 7 of Spades in the third row; the next cards will follow these, after having been shuffled, cut and drawn; the first will appear above in the spread to arrange the row for the others, in a series of 5. Everyone denotes what they see by their own accord; if it does happen, that these cards do not seem to imply anything in the row, reshuffle, cut and draw 5 new cards, which you will place below mentioned row, and you will explain that in the same way. There is money in thought, bad, wasted; money from the countryside; in the shape of a Lover, generous Lover, Love discarded; Lover a woman; in a lawsuit, Good, poor to nothing; You

---

[81] Translator: *bat,* i.e."beat" the cards. The modern French word is *melanger.*

on to the military. As you can see, this draw is
very easy to learn.

Draw of Fifteen

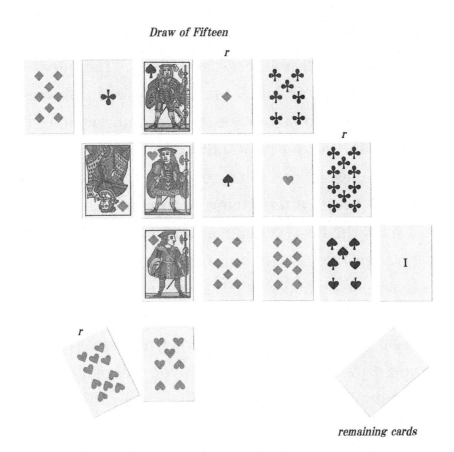

remaining cards

*Cards shown are the reproduced Provot from the 1790s. With kind
permission from the JC Flornoy Estate. www.tarot-history.com*

I had one of my Schoolchildren in the provinces, who with this single draw of which I made him feel the results, as I am going to go over it with you, confirm the most famous which appears; here it is expressed with an air of kindness: This card says Money, the other Lover, these two indicate a Trial[82]; and returning a moment later, I say choose 3 cards, he does not fail to pick one of the three, or sometimes two. By this method you would know, what the person is most fond of: We call that, asking people for what they want, in order to give them what they want.

---

[82] Translator: The money is implied by the the 7 of Clover, the 10 of Clover reversed is the lover, the 7 of Spades left of the Etteilla indicates trials.

Let's study the Horoscope. This Horoscope is
very different from all the others; but it is not
different from itself, since it is not possible to do
this otherwise, without being assured of its little
value. So you draw the cards, after shuffling, cut
as usual, then ask, in what month was I born? The
month of September; how many letters are there
in the month of September? 9 and if it was in
March, you would say 5; so you would go; 9 times
20 is 180, the quarter of that is 45, consequently
at just 45 you will obtain what the first 4 cards
meanings imply on this plan. Grief, Friendship,
Spirit and Mother[83]; you see that I use the meaning
of the first card, the secondary meaning of the
second, the meaning of the number for the third,
and the secondary of the number for the fourth:
So follow this approach until the end, go to the
bar of the Etteilla, see with this operation, on the
counter-base bar, if the pairing is agreeable and
if it still yields to you anything, at that specific

---

[83] Translator: Etteilla uses the 4 first cards on the horoscope draw.
The Ten of Spades is sorrows or grief. Friendship as a secondary
would be implied by a 7 of Spades. The Jack of Clover, no. 25, implies
Spirit as the primary meaning of the number. Mother is implied by the
Queen of Diamonds, no. 3, as the secondary meaning of the number.

age. The first card is the Eight of Hearts; the meaning is a blond girl; as a result you will cry over a blond girl.

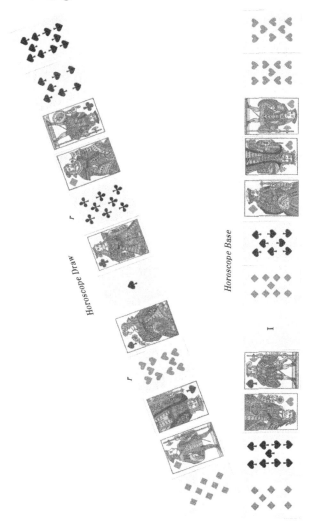

Cards shown are the reproduced Provot from the 1790s. With kind permission from the JC Flornoy Estate. www.tarot-history.com

Let us study the second, following this approach, it is the secondary meaning which we must consult; it tells us of boredom[84]; your friendship will be boring; the bar, as you can see, implies your friendship is a challenge.

Now let's look at the third card; the meaning of its no. is generosity[85]; the bar shows improvement, you will have a spirit of generosity, consequently be of good spirit; one can have a generous spirit without spending money, by helping through one's lights, with advice, the oppressed, the poor, the weak, the widow, the orphan. Let us see the secondary meaning of the number of the fourth card; it says Tutor;[86] your mother will need a Tutor. Is that all that will happen to you at 45? No, this is how you need to consult the rest; from the number 20 and the 12, and as you move forward one card at the time, you will see, that two rows meet in the Eight of Diamonds. I only see two Jacks in reverse which implies company; at 45 years of age you will be

---

[84] Translator: The 9 of Cups in reverse.
[85] Translator: The Jack of Cups, the no. 12.
[86] Translator: See footnote page 49.

the topic of society, that is to say you will meet many people. I don't see anything else at this age; let's move on: now you say 9 times 22 is 198, a quarter is 49 and a half years; you do the same operation for remaining 8 cards, leaving the first bar and you will see, what will happen to you at that specific age. So from card to card until the last one, follow well, what I have described for the first four; when you get to the ninth, you will take the secondary meaning of the number from the Ten of Spades, as well as the base bar, so in the end you have to find all meanings of the primary and secondary meanings of your 24 cards; you will not forget to pay attention to all the numbers as well, which you can easily do.

If by chance it has occurred that I or the print has a mistake, with a little reflection you will easily correct the fault, which in any case would not be of consequence for the instructions of this game, since you must know all the primary meanings and secondary meanings of your cards; so, as I said, you would do well in following this authors approach.

There are still, as everyone knows, many ways to entertain oneself in the game of guessing; but all of them should aim for fun, and prefer the ones, that relieve boredom the most, and which I believe to be the Etteilla, since there are an infinite number of combinations, each one more amusing than the next. But back to these other methods; they are in fashion, Taraux[87], tin or molten lead, the coffee marc, egg whites. The cards are no truer than all that; but at least one amuses oneself there with a more pleasant illusion and more taste.

---

[87] Translator: *The Tarot.*

Memory of this Woman

There are many things that I have not mentioned in my spreads; but there are some that I have implied, which you may find by deriving them from the many meanings. I play this game according with the time available.

I said she was disguised as a man, she was born in the middle of the countryside, on the edge of a river, her parents were from nobility, her father was dead, her mother remarried; she was put in a cloister, she got married; her parents abducted her, they journeyed together, they almost perished at sea, she became pregnant, gave birth to a boy; she was arrested and returned to the cloister; her parents abducted her a second time, took her to Paris, her husband tracked her down, fought with the lover; the lover withdrew, the woman went back to the cloister; her husband who held her there died, the mother of this young wife became interested in her, rescued her from the cloister; free, she asked for the grace of her lover, she obtained it; they met again; misery took them; she married a second time; the lover married

around the same time; she left her husband to join
her lover, they quarreled, and she separated from
him; she went back to live with a clerk, fell into
poverty, made some bad acquaintances; she was
led to a place by force; her husband claimed her,
she sent her children to her parents; a rich man
saw her, made her a proposal, which she accepted;
she fell in love with a servant, ruined the man who
did her good, enriched the lover who left her;
reduced to misery, she rediscovered an ancient
craft which fed her; went to the D ..... made parts,
became a woman of society; found a young Lord,
barely an adult, who went into debt for her, whose
family wanted her locked up; she registered for a
show with her lover; began there, was poorly
received; she left this spectacle, got married with
a provincial troop; left him, returned to the D. ...
could not do her business there; took a partner
from back home, with an old woman, dressed as a
stranger, and all three left for the countryside;
briefly roamed the provincial towns, was called a
Marquise widow; she found a lover, half ruined
him and came to Paris: ashamed of her life, she
devoted herself to gambling, the wins, the losses,

fought, had a lawsuit, won it, but at a cost; went to find her daughter, stayed with her, quarreled, sold all the furniture, and changed her name and neighborhood; her daughter's lover sent for her, she was found, pleaded to settle justice, won; reunited with her daughter, summoned her son; changed her customs and conduct; married off her daughter to a good merchant; put her son in the service, quarreled with everyone, went alone back to the provinces to find one of her lovers; returned to Paris, and left for a foreign Kingdom with him: this is where she is now; she is 39 years old, still a beautiful woman.

There are many singular events within this story: I could make an ongoing story; but that is not my talent; the shame she carries and the desires, she must keep quiet about, for the rest of her days, testify to us sufficiently, Reader, the remorse of having led a life without conduct. Farewell, Readers.

E N D.

Other book translations from the same author;

Tarot decks;

The Lemarchand tarot deck

The Z.Lismon tarot deck

Made in United States
North Haven, CT
04 February 2023

32035810R00068